*S*ecrets of the *W*ind

Robert L. Martin

Preface

This is my fifth book with Cyberwit.net. They all have made me very happy. The titles from the first to the current ones are: ***Wings of Inspiration, Rhymes of the Joke Machine, The Air Almighty, Martin's World,*** and this one, ***Secrets of the Wind.***

I wrote the poetry, my daughter Renata designed the covers, and my lady friend Linda helped with the illustrations. All of my books are available on Amazon and most of them are on Barnes and Noble.

If you have read the prefaces in my books, you have learned a little about me each time; where and how the words come to me, my thought process, and how much I love what I am doing. We senior citizens have to have a hobby, a regimental exercise routine, and something to look forward to besides our grandchildren to keep us thinking young. Life is worth striving to hold onto as long as we can make it last. We have so much more to do and learn.

Secrets of the Wind is again a collection of my poems, so far totaling 2,200 and counting. After I finish one poem, I get inspired to write another. Sometimes it is a segue leading to the next one. Sometimes it puts me into the mood to conjure up my deepest feelings in order to express my deepest thoughts and put them into the next poem. Sometimes I read some excerpts from Pablo Neruda's book, "The Essential Neruda." He and Kahlil Gibran are my inspirational mentors. Both elevate my thinking process so I can raise my own level of thought from their thoughts. I also get inspired when I listen to such composers as Igor Stravinsky, Jennifer Higdon, John Adams, Alberto Ginastera, and I love the pulse of rap and rock music. It is very moving and exciting.

I am very fortunate to be in the Barnes and Noble bookstore in Easton, PA and in their online system. They give me the opportunity to sign my books and participate in their functions. On my first book signing, Pastor John brought the whole church congregation down to buy my books. They were very impressed by it and invited me back. I am a very lucky man.

Acknowledgments

First of all, I would like to thank all of you who bought and read my previous books. Secondly, I also hope you liked them. I would like to thank my daughter Renata who designed the cover again like she did in all my books, and also J.T. and his wife Lisa for finding my old files that were hidden in my old laptop that crashed. Without them coming to the rescue, it would have taken much longer to write this book.

Below are listed all the publishers that gave me permission to use my poems that they published before.:

My poems ***The Disclosure, Requiem for a Soldier, The Dews of Autumn,*** and ***Ice*** were previously published by "The Belt and Beyond."

My poems ***Lord of the Seas*** and ***Love in the Autumn*** were previously published by "Poets' Espresso."

My poems ***Sea of Treachery*** and ***Outside Boy*** were previously published by "Madswirl."

My poems ***The Proud Violet*** and ***The Weeping Lyre*** were previously published by "Long Story Short."

My poem ***Cloud*** was previously published by "Blue Lake Review."

My poem ***Steam*** was previously published by "Oddball Magazine."

My poem ***That Special Night*** was published by "Wilderness House Literary Journal."

Contents

The Home of Balladry

The home of balladry, of the melodic wind,
the whistling trees,
the flutes of the forest nymphs,
the air that passes through the keys,
the magic air that breaks into pieces
into melodies that soothe the senses,
lullabies for the hard charging spirits,
the music in the glen,
the keeper of the sounds
locked away in cerebral vaults,
house of the wandering truths,
the poets in charge of the wandering,
the balladeers that push it along,
the dreamers that knead it and make it pliant,
that dress it up in the finest satin
and paint it in pastel colors,

the truth that keeps the house together
but runs with the nomadic spirit at times,
the un-taming of the tamed
that dances with the wild wind,
rides upon the drifting clouds,
and lives out the dysfunctional dreams,
while inventing new truths along the way,

and balladeers looking in the eyes of beauty
that form the sadness that
runs through their skin,
the tears of reverence flowing freely,

the silent prayers that come to them,
the altars they find in their silent depths
as they worship its divine nature
from the spontaneous psalms
running through their mind,

the sadness, the joy, the reverence,
the clarity, the elation, the intelligence,
the wisdom, the self-assuredness,
the heart and soul of the poets,
the seekers of divine wisdom,
the keepers of the words and sounds,
all in the mind of the balladeer,
the keeper of the home.

The Great Pacific

Up to the soaring eagle and back
down to the miniscule sea below,
site of wiry lines inching forth
before its eyes,
smiling at the sun and
basking in the quiet,
Neptunian galleries in the light,
nature's unassuming beauty on display,
a sight lodged in the eyes of the beholder,
a grand phenomenon in view
from far above the sea,
from the briny scent of nature's mantle,

as peace and disquietude roll in
from glassy columns and tempest risings
from the tales of the
colossal sea beast fanning in the deep,
building casual hills that
swell into mountains
and mountains shrinking
back into casual hills
that disappear upon the sandy shore,
another life under the life before the eyes,
an ancient mystery from the bowels of the sea
as nature rolls with the enigmatic tides,

the home of the Great Pacific,
its vastness of gigantic proportions,
its countless streams of water teeming,

its many moods showing their faces
of beauty and peril,
her terror, her reverence,
her strength, her weakness,
her quietude, her turbulence,
her assault upon the ships,
her white lines of steel
beating up the sandy shores,

but isn't beauty a many sided
display of charm and perplexity?

Secrets of the Wind

Ancient Gods at home in their secret hideaways
lords of the wind and conductor of its fate
all powerful in mind, body, and deeds
creator and designer of the currents
surveyors at work a million and nine miles
'neath the threshold of heaven
staking out the boundaries that
 separate the hot from the cold
with rivers that flow between the elements

keeping the esoteric origin of the winds
a deep secret sealed up in their vaults
keeping out of the view of humanity
to be divulged when
all divine revelations come to light

but for now a quixotic poem of the poets
 the masseurs that massage the intellect
a melting down of the words into a sigh
a sigh that disrupts the flow of anxiety
a dam made out of consecrated steel
a psalm that opens the doors of the divine
a look into the face of the heavens

a secret that teases the impatient mind
a revelation at the time of death
a reward for the inquisitive and virtuous minds
and a secret that reveals itself
through a visual encounter through the eyes
and not just from the rustling of the leaves.

Water

Water, dews of heaven, of sacred clouds,
of ancient origins, pliant cathedrals, teary doors,
sympathetic hearts, observant eyes,
mother of the weeping meadows,
heroine of the parched fields,
matriarch of the Divine Order,
Lady Power, Lady Mercy, Lady Gentle,
fed by the lava from the volcanoes of peace,
Gods of kindness and compassion,
water flowing from its hallowed home of purity,
anointed by the scepter of the Supreme,

and water, the child of the bestial tempest
with its black and whirling colossal wings,
the materialization of the diabolic mind,
the marauder of the quiet earth,
the hater of the peaceful life,
the sweat of the father of the infernal order,
the venom streaming from his mouth,
the hell that's formed upon the seas,
upon the gentle earth, the wheat fields,
the altars of the human spirit
and their hopes and dreams,
taking lives down under,
down, down to the
bottoms of the Earth.

Waters holy and waters evil;
eternal waters of random desires,
flowing to their predetermined destinies.

Sway

Swaying, drifting, new silence down under,
quiet dancing in the rivers of the seas,
aquatic gardens, nautical flowers bending,
artistic moving with influential currents,
touching but not touching,
feeling the air of their air,
feathered waters encompassing,
swaying to the maestro's baton,
the motion of the waters,
the art of synchroneity in full cadence,
poetic motion singing to the tides,
dancing to the rhythms of their silent drums,
beauty in motion, beauty in its easy drifting,
enraptured by the poetic movements,
drifting in the world down under
unseen by human eyes
where the tallest flowers grow
and rise to catch the motion of the waters,
the hidden rivers that flow inside
where the secrets of the deep stay hidden,
where beauty floats in its ancient chambers,
too shy to rise and flaunt its beauty,
such beauty wasted in its secret depths,
oh such beauty of the poetic waters.

Wind & Seas

Power supreme and power of a sigh,
power of the tides and of the wind
 that moves the waves,
and power that pushes beauty
through the fissures of the skin
and down to the heart and soul
and performs its magic that
stimulates the internal organs
and dances upon the surface of the skin
and in the depths of the eyes
that acknowledge the
wonderment of beauty,

and the beauty of the crest of the waves,
the saintly white colored churning that
rolls to the shore like a poetic dream,
then sinks back into the calm again
to gather up like it did before and becomes
a part of another crest to run ashore,

power supreme that is all powerful,
those earthly eternal mechanics that remained
the same since the blueprint of the oceans
that were drawn up at the time of creation,
 from the all-powerful mind of the creator,
the mastermind behind nature's execution
that can overturn the ships or also
make the passageway as smooth as silk,

the wind, the seas, the God of might,
 the father of us all,
the impenetrable wall that stands firm
as we test its strength, durability,
 and credibility,
the Father God that loves us and
shows us what strength is,

the nature that makes us revere its nature,
the power that shows us what power is,
the teacher that makes us feel his lessons,
the lessons that lead us the shores of wisdom,
the wisdom that shows us the wall
and that we cannot penetrate it,

an ode to the wind and seas,
their power and might,
the wall that they create,
their poetic movement,
the poem that they inspire in us,
oh yes, the eternal wind and seas.

Of Whispering Winds

Of whispering winds and dismantled trees
come melodies split into harmony and creeds;
secret argots sung by the forest winds,
bending sounds through the barren limbs.

Winter's etude is on the tongues of the balladeers
 by the mothers of sorrow of the spilling tears,
the unforgiven haunting of which can't be controlled
through the force of nature let the lore be told,
evoking the exodus of the emerald-colored leaves,
a song of lament is in winter's paralyzing freeze.

The Reign of Melody

Melody, strange lady endowed with absolute powers
leaning over the meadows from the highest towers
she of might and tenderness and melodic smiles
soft velvet tears and hypnotic guiles

ranks over the powers of man, royalty, and kings
from gentle melodies flowing with all it brings
and rhythm that moves the arms and legs
with ammo begotten from internal powder kegs

melody of a smile and melody of a cathartic rant
running wild in the voice of a full-hearted chant
or a song of a violet enclaved by a luxurious grove
seeking solace from the stony winds that blow

beautiful melodies, movers of stationary souls
heartener of warriors to their triumphant goals
or speakers in the silence of a murmuring brook
or the pounding of the tempest as the earth hath shook

an ode to music and her stirring melodies
and how she reigns over sententious bodies
over souls of monarchs, of kings and queens
with a song for them and what she sings

Lord of the Seas

If only I could rule the motion and the tides,
the temperance of the skies,
wrap the clouds around my mind, my soul,
stand above the waves, the wrath,
 the upheaval of the underground,
the diabolic floors, the deep sea spirits,
subdue the churning of the waters,
the works of the capricious twisters,
the children of the Lords of the Dark,
hovering over the broken rhythms
of the rolling waves,
smashing and overturning its own columns
with its grayish colors at war with each other,
 playing with the ships and
 singing war chants in its acts of demolition,
exercising their power over the sea,
all in a day in the life of the children of the Dark.

The time has come to disrupt
their devilish escapades, their fun with the ships,
 smooth out the tumultuous waves and
make the passage way safe again as it was before;
the time to reprimand the deeds of the tempest,
to blow them away with my all powerful breath,
my own wind from my own secret arsenal,
then reach down and lift up the ships,
knead their iron clad bottoms,
feel their terror-stricken tears in my fingers,
sing a soothing lullaby to them
and send them on again to their designated port,
all in a day in the life of the Lord of the Seas.

Deep Sea Underground

Days of yore when the moon was a
 mystic sphere, a quixotic poem for lovers,
a silver private island in the sky
  encased in the finest porcelain as
the heads of colossal benevolent ghosts
appeared looking out into deep space
while scanning the Universe,
looking for the lost ships and
drawing the tides up with their tearful eyes,
it was the underground of the upper skies.

Now man has felt the moon ground under his feet
that became no longer a poem of lovers,
but a grounding of their imagination,
too familiar to suspend them in the air,
and too heavy to keep them afloat.

But under the skies and the earth and the waters
where virgin land is yet virgin territory,
and the fishes are outer-world swimmers
swimming near the floors of the
world of the unseen,
where life is yet a poem for lovers,
we can swoon again and let our imagination
take us to exotic places in our minds
and keep our spirits high with
a poem of the deep sea underground,
penned by the sonnateers
of our hearts.

Melodic Fingers

Rousing spine from soft melodic fingers
left in the trail and such as music lingers
when it sings so softly as a muted feather
reveling in the melody for ever and ever

floating in deep space and so beyond
propelled by the wave of a magic wand
magic blessed by the Gods of music
the purifiers and softeners of all the rhetoric

those with music impacted in their hearts
 permission to leave as the sound embarks
from melodic fingers dancing on the keys
playing melodies into a soft ocean breeze

music floating on the crest and swells
and in the ringing of the celestial bells
up and down the spines of the music lovers
in the spirit of the sound that closely hovers

the rites of the quixotic mind in force
the rousing of the tired spirit at the source
 power to the blood to the fingers to the tips
in the veins of clarity as the mood befits

ecstasy of sound and joy and power
rainbow glitter and stardust shower
melodic fingers dancing on a cloud
and chanting to the upper skies aloud,
"Music oh music, how sublime thou art."

A Ballad in Space

Of beauty cast out in the mystic space,
of music with wings and whiter lace,

a ballad above the clouds in a lighter list,
rolling with the motion of the surrounding mist,

sweet music from the pipes of the cherubim,
higher up than where the whirly winds begin,

a song of effervescence and passion flowing,
and harmony keeping the song forever growing,

clusters of sound swirling with the winds of time,
and rhythms pushing the music into a sea of rhyme,

as beauty prides herself amidst the crimson clouds,
flaunting her colors so much as heaven allows,

and music climbs the sky to a nocturnal star,
and takes its sweetness up to a land so afar,

in satchels of perfume and exotic spice,
to a heaven called music and paradise,

and sits upon a throne in the glorious kingdom,
a landing of the song, a melodic venturesome,

a lullaby to the busy skies and swirling winds,
a breath of heaven in sound by violins,
a ballad to put to sleep the fury of the skies.

Highway to Bliss

Rocky roads left behind and forgotten
melted down into white satin
by the breath of the southern wind
  suface lined with rainbow dust
 smoothing miles up ahead
melodious currents in the skies
aero cushions floating in space
feathered landings on the stars
language of the spheres in the heart
the safety of the mind in the paladium
listless riding on soothing wings
quiet wind with hallowed hands behind
breath of heaven against the earnest sails
pure heart beating with every mile
destination engraved on the forehead
running down to the spine the heart the soul
the taste of bliss on the carnal tongue
a hallowed bliss that permeates the senses
an allurement that draws heaven nearer
a landing that has no words to say
 a wonderment a jubilation a sigh just the silence - -

- -

The Appeasement

Crispy azure firmament, visions of paradise,
of clarity, of ecstatic dreams, of regal heritage,
of mythical cathedrals suspended in the blue,
beatitudes for the quixotic eyes,
floating gardens of copious blue roses,
angelic corridors lined with blue satin,
spacious avenues to the Kingdom up ahead,

appeasing skies from the hell left behind
when the seas were heaving columns of liquid steel,
spume of the skyborne beast,
violent declamations of the maddened tempest,
of a language flowing out of the
 slithering nervous black clouds
aimed at the peaceful waters down below,
stirring up their synchronous motion
generated by the smooth aquatic
 engines of the deep,
disturbing the rhythmic peace of the swells,
in a northward flowing
 at battle with the eastward,
the hell from down under surfacing
to deface the easy passageways of the ships,

such a sight in the corridors to heaven
after the hell hath raged,
of Hurricane Ian falling apart in the peaceful sky
and blending in with the beauty of it,
and of him apologizing for the evil done

for smashing the Floridian homes,
and him being driven by
more powerful forces,

proving that the path of evil
leads to peaceful results,
of appeasement repairing harsh feelings,
of love letting in the divine peace
to take over the resentment in the heart.

Cloud

Of your artistic shapes and moods,
pictorial playground of the azure skies,
lofted oceans and soft white waves,
home of dreams and imagination,
where riders ride on white stallions,
with scepters pointing to the firmament,
with plumes of silken rivulets trailing,
your cottony faces and contented smiles,
your protruding chest of pure white silk,
your proud submission to the sacred winds,
 your moods propelled by the heat of the day
and the cold, cold northern winds,
your love affair with the mad tempest,
singing with the thunder,
dancing with the lightning,
binding with the heated passion,
twisting through the black and gray
until you weaken and grow tired,
kissing the feet of the angels in the blue,
riding on the smiles of the rainbow,
the handiwork of the almighty,
dancing the "Dance of the Zephyrs,"
the returning to the soft winds
and their fragrant breath,
a child of their earthly authority,
in love with the ever shifting skies,
and the permanence of the heavens,
the almighty's land above all else,
above Mother Nature's home

on the outskirts of heaven,
ever shifting, riding, floating,
moving, dancing, waiting, smiling,
changing, drifting……………

Rhymes of the Wind

Rhymes of the wind
Whistling through the forest,
Air of the north passing through,
An ode to winter's touch,
Her soft alighting, mass assemblage,
Her vistas, her charm, her milk,
An ardent poem
Composed by the breath of the north,
Shaped by the
 Arms of the trees,
A language of a thousand tongues,
The voice of the empyreal,
Universal psalms,
Hidden poems within a poem,
An ode to the passing of the seasons,
Summer's charm giving into winter
Stripped of its emeralds that
Lay waste on the forest floor,
Taking on a new texture,
A new sonnet of the seasons,
A new poetry of the new age
Reciting winter's lament,
A requiem for the death of the old
And a euphoric ode to the new
In a language of the spirits
Wrapping around the trees of the forest,
Speaking to the ear of the heart,
The rhymes of the wind,
The lore of the forest
From the poetry of
The voices of the seasons.

Steam

Your sensual moves, your massive powers
 Your primal sorcery, your sunken towers
Your steamy stories at nature's playground
Rising from the north going southward bound

You fly out of volcanoes like frightened birds
Like hungry lions chasing scattered herds
You add power to power and speed to speed
Going to places where all adventurers lead

In the face of beauty you ascend to the highest
Where eagles take flight and build their nest
You flood the heart with a passion's brew
You turn a wise man into a bewildered fool

You rise up from tombs with your banners blazing
You offer to the spirit sweet nectar's glazing
Life is a bitter planet touched by frozen hands
A spot reserved by fate where passion lands

You hover over wedding beds with the softest wings
Reciting love's heated ritual with a spirit that sings
You scatter seeds and hope that love is growing
As wild rivers from quiet streams in their flowing
You are life as you move into new places
You are the steam that gives life to all faces

Affinity

Heaven's magic, wizard's brewing
Power supreme, spirits moving
Focal point is a second ahead
When love becomes a story unsaid

Magnets power as tides ebb and flow
Attraction pulls as love becomes aglow
Silent poems pour out of hidden places
Where nature works with heaven's graces

Two strangers arrive at love's eternal gate
Together under the spell of a mystifying fate
Affinitive charms in their perpetual blooming
Roses and spices and searing currents fluming

The throne of love is a place called bliss
Where spirits rise for a consummated kiss
Volcanoes rumble while love commands
Two lovers have fallen into nature's hands

An ode to affinity, an ode to its calling
Its powers relentless, its voices enthralling
The magic of attraction and how it works
Two lovers perplexed as the loving perks

Two lovers plunging into love's sacred fire
Taking love up higher and higher
As heaven waits upon their ascension
The book of love and its serious intention
To the glory of love I
Give myself unto thee

Surface Magic

Magicians at the outer edges,
of soothing lines and liquid gold,
enchanted forests
of mystic dreams,
of beauty in the glassy lakes,
alluring arms
of mythical nymphs,
bringing eyes and hearts
to the surface abound
with entries stationed
at the glossy gates,
shielding them from
entering inside
and finding the truth
that lies within,
the house of the beast,
the face that hides in the midst
of mechanical smiles
and plastic tears,
disconnected from the
outer edges,
the ingredients of the soul
of a manufactured beauty
far below the dazzling surface.

"Beware gentlemen
of the new order,
you among the
rest of humanity,

hopeless judges of the
good and bad,
enraptured by the glossiness
trapped in the arms
at the surface,

find your way out and
look at the beauty again
and see its internal bewitchery.

Gorgeous

Crested beauty she floats on the air,
Intoxicating sweetness our lady fair,
The sky her yard and clouds her home,
Perfumed trails where she hath roamed.

Through dark forests and sunlit trails,
Over golden peaks then tender swales,
Transforming the ground as she softly treks,
Blessing the earth with her sainted steps.

Beauty left alone is beauty undefiled,
As we gaze into the heavens all the while.
One touch is a million hands all over.
Purity is a fragile flower in the clover.

She is Venus alive with a beating heart,
A step above the embellishment of art.
When the future kissed the dew of the morn,
She arose with the sun from Gabriel's horn.

Her eyes straight ahead affixed in her trance,
Who knows the story with just one glance?
Joy and sadness are written on her face.
Secrets hide beneath her black satin lace.

Life she has at her manicured fingertips.
Winning the smiles from trembling lips.
She is gorgeous as she passes by,
Flaunting beauty in her stride.
She is what men die for,
If they could ever touch.

Bee & Flower

Pleasure, the ecstasy of the senses,
the attraction, beauty embodied
and reaching out
in obedience to the holy commands
to humanity and creatures of the land
   driven by ecstasy and pleasure,
the laws of propagation mandated and obeyed,

the sensations in the organs in the bodies
 of the bees and humans running alike
in the face of beauty,
and to the bee,
 the alluring flowers in the meadow,
the fountain of life to get inside
and bask in its loveliness,
to flow in the rivers of aphrodisia,
and touch the loin for its revival,
to answer to nature's sweet calling,
a joyful submission to the calling,
the sweet arms of love reaching out
and placing us into the lap of love,
letting us feel the intimacy and pleasure
and feel the texture of heaven,

to the bee and to us,
 answering to the call of pleasure,
to the flower, the yielding of the honey,
the joyful response to the passion of the bee,
the messenger from heaven who gave it life,
the holy union of bee and flower,
nature at work as her sacred duties.

Perfume

When she passed by, the scent was heaven
Moving in the air and running through the glen
A summer's wind climbed through the vines
Drenched in heavenly brews and tasty wines

The romantic that I am, came to be smitten
A love story of my life about to be written
Love's aroma has beckoned me to follow
To the ends of the earth, my secret hollow

She is a poetic dream dressed in red roses
Of love coming down in heavenly doses
A potpourri of her and love bound potions
And me swimming in perfumed oceans

I will arise with her lying down at my side
My dream to make her my beautiful bride
My dying wish is to keep that scent forever
To linger through my years
And all what lies beyond

Of Sight And Guile

She blows in from boreal hideaways,
From homes with no names,
From frigid deserts and black sands,
From dark caves and musty tombs,
From witches' huts and fragrant brews,
From serpents' dens and beastly shapes
From Medusa's touch and passion's heat,
From inferno's fire and dancing flames,
From hell's tolling and open gates.

She with her flailing skirts, white thighs,
Private flashings, magnetic sightings,
Luscious peaks, mysterious valleys,
Melting curves, wayward roads,
Silky skin, soft fingers, dancing arms,
Floating feet, starry eyes, holy face,
Liquid love, mobile truths,
Burning language, throbbing loins,
Cunning smiles, exoteric charm,
Plastic tears, paper hair,
Leather soul, and metal heart,
On a mission of destruction,
Moves into the hearts of fools.

Superficial beauty is a spectacle
That hides its content.
True beauty is a spectacle
That represents its content.

The Wings Of Love

Deep crimson wings drifting in the skies,
As heaven looks down with its loving eyes,

At one lover alone and one heart incomplete
Acting in compliance to fill that empty seat

Found a young maiden of twenty long years
Fulfilled his dreams as his loneliness disappears

Took to the hallowed air to heaven's dominions
A bizarre flight with swords hidden in the pinions

On wings of oblivion and wings of pure bliss
He lost himself for the feel of heaven's kiss

Navigated stormy rivers and floated in rivulets
Dragged thru' the coals and over thrilling sunsets

Where he found the secret of his virgin heart
That beat away the solitude in a broken shard

For the crowning of love and its crucifixion
He marched toward its heart in curious submission

He found that world of passion in its wild nature,
His losing himself in the throes of laughter,
His crying with the agony of a wounded bird,
And his rolling with life without a binding gird.

Where the wings of love transported his soul,
With tears of compassion to make his life whole,
He landed where love prescribed for him to land,
In the life of love where lovers band.

Suzie Wonder

Little baby Suzie and her big pink rattles,
her constant crying and her vernacular battles,
her wonderment with her new found toys,
her inherited smiles and ensuing joys,

her doll houses with pretty pink shutters,
her dolls responding to everything she mutters,
they're wearing big girls' attire with all the curves
like the big girls she knows while she observes.

Her new clothes made for how Suzie looks,
are what she sees in catalogs and books.
How to catch the eyes of an on-looking boy,
she learns how many egos she can destroy.

Her schooling is a place of never learning,
the right place to be for her constant yearning;
academics of love and all that she'll need,
learning the wiles of love and how to succeed.

She lifted up her skirts is what she did
and watched the on-lookers, heaven forbid.
Showing her innocence, but gloating in her charm
she moved about in the most revealing garb;

then moved on to the imperial ranks of royalty
with her alluring smiles and looking all so pretty,
romancing kings and becoming influential,
our innocent little Suzie of newly acquired guile.

Using her appeal to dethrone such foolish kings
in the wake of her affairs and all her flings,
she's all equipped to rule the world.
She's all grown up to be a big, big girl.

The Ring

"Around your finger, your beautiful finger,
Your empty one that makes my spirit linger,

Your poetic movements of swanlike gestures,
Of melodic heavenly moonlight overtures,

Your beautiful finger, your orchestral baton,
Your lineation of beauty and then beyond,

Your dancing spirit that wraps around me
And pulls me into your mysterious sea,

Your beautiful finger that extends from you,
Where beauty grows, beauty holds true,

Your parts unadorned are parts to me adored,
A shrine before my eyes for now and evermore.

Beauty stirs up the blemishes with a magic potion,
An enchanting mixture beneath the mystic ocean.

Your everything is the embodiment of bliss
As I would die to be for one eternal kiss,

To be smothered by your overwhelming limbs,
From a life not lived to where pleasure begins,

To where two divinities create a third to be born
Under the auspice of the divine as duly sworn.

Upon thy lovely finger, would you accept my ring?
To complete my life and make my heart sing?

Would you pledge your love to me as I do to you?
My darling, I love you more and more every day.
Please marry me, my beloved."

Daughter Of Passion

Listen for the silent sound of passion,
The sound that starves for your silent touch.
Raise your bow in reverence to the
Gods of music and blend into their lead.
When they send fire to you, fuel it with your fire.
When they send sadness to you, give them yours.
When they send tenderness, caress it with love.
You are a slave and the music is your grand master.
Bring that beautiful and fragile neck
And gently place it under your chin, as violinists do.
Get ready to glide your bow across the strings,
As if not touching, but yet still touching,
Like a vampire drifting up the castle walls.
Dive into the music and swim with the current.
Bring your all with you and leave nothing behind.
Shed your tears and let them drip into the flow,
Daughter of tears of hidden love.
Hold on to that sensual sound as if
Music was about to run away forever,
And you are saving its burning embers.
Hold on to life as if life was tired of living.
 Put yourself in the way as heroines do.
Keep the music flowing with the sound of tears.
They are the spark and you are the inspiration.

I've fallen deeply in love with you,
Daughter of passion and messenger of sound.
In my reveries, we are passionate lovers.
I can see us dancing across the bridge.

I see your eyes as they melt into your heart.
Every tear tells a story of joy and pain.
You are a book that pulls me in deeper,
As each page is a journey into the unknown.
You paint a picture of hallowed spaces
As they come forth and reveal themselves,
Sound of color, sound of shapes, sound of clarity.
I love the way you bend with the music as it
Kneads you and prepares you for the sacred fire.
You are a flame that keeps it going.
Music is your mother and
You are the Daughter Of Passion.

Jack-hammer Lullaby

Bang, crash, blam, rat-a-tat tat,
slam, bam, whop, crunch, whap!!!

Lullaby like the snow so gently falling,
like floating in the air soft voices calling.
Sleep me little baby to the soothing sound,
a silent lullaby with euphony all-around.

Kapow, kablam, ouch, rattle, jam,
nerve racking, crashing, wham, bam!!!

So soothing to the ear so soft and sweet
in keeping pace with the feathering beat,
of muted drums in calico sunsets
o'er lazy hillocks and bubbling rivulets.

Ouch, son-of-a, slam, flam, whang,
the earth hath shooken, the thunder rang,
teeth shaking, banging, whipper slay!!!
Jack-hammer lullaby with me forever stay.

Oh lovely melody flowing in my heart,
a lazy sonnet to an ascending Lark,
angelic wings in their flapping
softly in my quiet napping,
oh sweet sounding
 oh sweet pounding,
sleep, sleep. sle-e-e-p -

- - - - - - - - - - - - - - -

Jack the Cap Captain

Spirit of Captain Jack hovering over me,
captain of the bottle caps brigade is he.
He twists the frigg'n cap to the right
when left I try to twist'n fight.

A whammy is what he sent to me on call
or a voodoo pin from his voodoo doll.
He tightens the caps so nobody can drink.
He's up to his shenanigans so I think.

Is he a nice spirit or a not so nice one?
Was he born in the womb or a mausoleum?
Maybe his mother came from the Isle of Hades
and he emerged from the coals all ablaze.
 Was it his idea to tighten the bottle caps,
or did it come from a herd of evil cats?
Doesn't he want us to taste his brew,
to turn his cap leftward to unscrew?
Maybe he's captain of a Tighten up Contest
and I'm a contestant in complete distress.
He turns to the right when I want to go left.
 OK. I give up. I did my best.

He's the cap captain of the cap brigade,
the nasty guru above the cavalcade,
too much for me to battle with,
so, I guess I'll just go thirsty therewith.

To hell with him.
But maybe he was there when it all began.

Unsainted

Standing before the tainted altar,
the unhallowed temple of the beast
from the chapel of pleasure,
adorned with red and black windows,
with gargoyles protruding from the walls,
serpents slithering through each other,
red canopies high above the rumpled sheets,
blood of the slaughtered lambs
dripping down upon naked bodies,
bed of the orgies and assorted debauchery,
slaves of love's lunacy,
disciples of Sodom and Gomorrah,
lovers of the other side of love,
of random lust of human flesh,
the letting loose of pleasure
into the sweaty pits of hell,
of sainted wells made unsainted,
of unholy waters flowing into
the devil's lot,

the enrollment of the chosen ones
of the disciples of the Anti-Christ,
the formal ritual of the zealous hearted,
the approaching to the altar
with open palms and open heart,
the kneeling down in devotion,
in allegiance to the mighty one,
the hot blooded sultan of evil,
the advocate of pleasure above all,

the one who defies all goodness,
whose every word is of
spite and debauchery,
the man with the face in the fire,
the man with seven horns,
the man above all men,
of pleasure granted
and righteousness defiled,
an alliance with the Sultan of Evil.

Losing of the Self

Swiftly how love runs among many courses,
Like a ride upon the backs of wild horses,

Affinity's protocol handed down to all lovers,
Each moment in line for all the others,

A sighting, a rush, a bewilderment, a joy,
A unifying force for Mother Nature to employ,

A reaction to how she works her magic,
And how it travels throughout so quick,

A submission to that force as love emerges,
The need to satisfy those unrelenting urges,

A burning desire to feel the heat of love,
To jump into the sacred fire from above,

A losing of the self and casting aside the fear,
Of the fire building and the pain so near,

A passion unattended from love's command,
A breath-taking trip to an exotic wonderland,

And the desire to live in that eternal place,
And to wake up with the dawn of beauty's face,

An ode to affinity and how it works,
And thank God for all it does.

The Fast Lane

Life in the fast lane,
full speed ahead,
as gazelles leap over time,
cheetahs outrun the thunder.
We bulldoze through iron walls,
hit the hitters and race the racers,
fly over mountains,
leap over fences and fence the leapers,
arrive before the lightning
hits the ground,
step on toes and fingers
and feelings and dreams
and smiles and violets.

We get there before the ominous clouds,
before the tempest curses the glassy seas.
We get there before the pouring rain,
before the heavy waves smash the rocks,
before they sink back into the angry waters,
before the rainbow smiles at the ships,
before the falling sun hits the horizon,
the crimson light shines into the night,
and the night casts its shadow on the earth.

We reach the golden years
before Father Time knows who we are,
before he arrives at our domicile,
before he knocks at our door,
before he begins to dig into us,

before he pulls out our sprightly spirit,
our enthusiastic climb to the future.
He brings the hereafter
to our contented homes,
the funeral plans and the eulogies,
the flowers and the tears
and the night before the day.
He pushes us up ahead as we
stop to look at the roses in the garden.
He wipes out our progressive steps
as we climb into the future.
Father Time, go home and come back later.

Air on Fire

Torches burn in the daylight time
 from the ire of the sun and air combined.
Dog days entrench in summer's fare,
as August heats up without a care.

The tropics begin their northern travels
as the steady current up high unravels.
They disrupt the flow while settling in,
in favor of a new climate to begin.
The air is on fire and nothing we can do,
so we get up and jump in the water pool.

Angel Fire

Galleries aloft in the majestic skies,
fire strewing through the perforated clouds,
doves spreading their colossal wings,
shooting fireballs from their electric eyes,
strafing artillery from the hallowed arsenals,
aiming at the barren earth, the cold tundra,
the shivering bones, the callous faces,
the empty hearts, the lonely arms,

throwing lovers together in an ambrosial web,
emptying out all earthly thoughts from them,
lifting their feet off the cold, cold ground,
shocking them with that magic vibration
that carries them from a world of weights
into a world of floating dreams,

or spits upon the parched forests
and spreads its venom to all lands near by
as it ravages everything in its path,
that beautiful flame so deadly.

Angel fire, the good and the bad,
the evil, the holy, the sacred, the infernal,
the wild, the tamed, the elegant beast,

that enigmatic flame that burns
wherever it so desires.

Air & Melody

Air and melody, sweetness and sorrow
encompassed by magestic wreaths of laurel

tears of silent valor and sound embellished
of air passing through the haunting mist

 velvet lullabies wrapped in purple violets
the autumn of light in the blushing sunsets

running thru' the night until the new day born
a song to the heavens as the skies all form

an ode to the passing day and day to come
an air of delight of the exalting sun

a melody supported by the air of the cherubims
like the divine morning dew as the day begins

the aroma of the sweetest rose gardens up high
an exotic language emitted by a pleasing sigh

a melody flowing out of the enchanted forests
a song in the air of the love-sick possessed

a passing through the glen, a lullaby of sorrow
a dirge from the swamps, an ode to tomorrow

melodies of circumstances and air of many moods
from the joys of living and the moaning of the blues

melody, a sound of sorrow and sound of joy
the air, a place for a dream and its wakening devoid

Elements of Music

Air and melody a potpourri of sound
a mixture of sweetness all around
of jasmine permeating the absorbent air
and melody running through an earnest prayer

melodious psalms in harmony with the wind
praising the earth and sky therein
carrying secrets of the life upon the earth
and the stories of how they spawned at birth

air without melody is air trapped in a vacuum
a space needed for whence they commune
like man and woman to keep life alive
fueling their desires to survive

sweet, sweet air, sweet melodies afloat
dormant feelings risen up and awoke
the rites of revelry sounded by trumpets
from eastern skies and the blazing sunsets

air and melody, the two combined
like the sun and rain by visionary design
air alone without music within
 a melody without room to rise up and spin
an ode to music and the life of it

Laughing Waters

Playground of the devil,
submissive waters from the docile air,
emptied of all emotion and energy,
weakened by the calming skies,
children of the Neptunian Commoners
nestled in the wombs in the
mothers of the sea,
homebodies with no spirit of adventure,
the ideal grounds for the mad tempest
to attack and wreak havoc,

to reach down inside the stillness
of the waters and their passive demeaner,
to light a fire under their feet,
to give them something inside to
fill the void of emotions
and instill in them a devilsh spirit,
a feeling of something other than nothing,
a new life to replace the old.

From the tempest hovering above,
home of the spirit of the devil
comes the perdition of the holy waters,
the stillness made tumultuous,
 angelic waters made bestial,
bestial made devilish,
devilish made mischievous
mischievous made playful,
playful made boisterous,

 boisterous made corrupt,
corrupt made whimsical,
whimsical not caring about the
state of the waters at the surface,
how the easy motion is disrupted,
laughing when the waves
battle with each other,
when they toss the ships around
and turn the still waters into
a playground of the devil
in obedience to the Lords
of the Netherworld.

Jet Stream Rogues

Jet stream rogues of the commanding seasons,
children of the manic tempest at play,
snaking their own way
through the yielding skies,
breaking ranks and running amuck
with a mind of their own,
rolling in the skies and laughing at the
uniformity of the seasons
and their regimental functioning;
the snowing in the season of snowing
and the blistering sun in its proper season,

rebels against the sun and the way
the earth rolls around it,
trying to alter the rotation,
the unyielding motion that began
when Mother Earth saw her first light.

With arms too weak and mind too capricious,
they are chased away by the
 eternal power that propels the seasons.

They are only temporary and led by the
whimsical mood of the restless air.
They are fools that fool only fools.

August Concerto

Orchestral sounds
from August fields,
droning choirs of
creatures small,
of crickets in the
rite of passion,
laying down a tone
for a concerto,
the calling for an
upcoming theme,
an overlaying of
melodic lines,
a blending of
cries and echoes,
a prelude to the
sounds of the birds
from their
lofted orchestral pits,
their nocturnal and
diurnal hymns,
night into day into
night into day,
the unassuming sophistication
that builds from
the August fields,
the droning, the blending,
the bending, the resonance,
the refining, the music,
Mother Nature's swan song

before the whistling of the
frigid winds between
the naked branches
of the naked trees
of winter,
an August concerto
composed by creatures
small and smaller,
nature's unassuming
orchestral members.

Pride of the Laborer

Work hard young man and young lady.
Go to the vineyards for the grapes are ready.
The time is now to harvest which you've sown.
Toil in the field until it's time to go home.

Pride in your work makes labor so much fun.
Your wages are minor, your dignity number one.
Work hard and feel the love guide you along,
for labor is a good deed and a joyful song.
As you bind yourself with other lovers of labor,
you feel the grace of God and do yourself a favor.
For hard work is grueling and all so menacing,
so approach it with love and a song to sing.

Utopia Fields

Final breath but air of hallowed truths,
a life to a new life,
an old body left behind but a
supernal body traveling on a highway
to bliss garnished in star dust,
a freedom ride to a greater freedom,
intelligence and Nirvana combined,
flowing into the consciousness,
riding on the rapids of speech,
 global language on the tongue,
global understanding in the mind,
global thoughts as one thought,
a knowledge of the whole
while journeying through space,

the fields of Utopia, a busy thoroughfare,
but an empty space in the eyes,

a landing upon the distant shores,
the threshold of the promised land,
the deliverance of all supplications
and all slaves of the truth rewarded
 as all the devoted ones shall be,
 merited from the wings of death
for the erection of the Utopian Universe
in the mind and in all matter.

Vicarious Dreams

Fathers at the head of the righteous home
in future's land where the seed is sown,
passing down morals from inside his heart,
pass them to his children to leave his mark.

The rights amended from his regretful wrongs,
a place achieved where the mind belongs,
he wishes to make them follow his dreams
and see himself running through the streams.

His new life lived through their own desires,
all the rightful deeds that contentment requires,
he lives inside and pulls the right strings,
the visionary ones that give them wings.

They soar to the highlands of their virtuous minds,
sailing through the mist as the beacon shines,
as father guides them through the streams
to the place described in his vicarious dreams.

The Disclosure

Along the road to Martin's Winding
before the season of mythical finding,
when Summer bleeds into Autumn's veins
and sheds its green as it slowly wanes,
discloses the mystery behind her delicate veils,
that no longer hide the quixotic myths and tales.

No more mystery of the secluded witch's homes,
the romping of the forest nymphs and gnomes;
no more imagines when the swelling thickets undo,
for all is disclosed and known to be true.
The veil is lifted as the leaves lay on the ground
and the mystery behind the greenery runs aground.

The Dews of Autumn

Autumn nights and summer days
Valleys covered in a morning haze
September air of night time sinking
Upon the grasses for the drinking

Hot and cold air, an autumn mix
Magicians in the clouds of assorted tricks
Casting their magic upon the earth
A time to play and a time of mirth
On the grounds of Sorcerer's Paradise
As the dews of autumn turn to ice.

Touching Rainbows

Tempest furor and skies bleeding oceans
Mother Nature concocting rebellious potions

Black clouds touching jagged mountain peaks
The angry skies at war as the thunder speaks

Sermons on the mount as nature curses the devil
Rising out of hell ascending up to heaven's level

As the mighty stands above the crowd to be heard
A hush among the boisterous, the calming word

Blue in the sky full of rainbows in their floating,
Now cover the firmament with a sumptuous coating,
Of red velvet tapestries with blue and yellow gold.
Beauty is hanging out in space to unfold.

Climb up and touch her smooth, electric surface
And feel the splendor that nature left on purpose.
As tempests climb into the sky and come to be,
They shed their fury and then go out and leave.

Mother Nature is a lady of sincere restitutions,
Her torturous pounding with quiet evolutions,
Her tumultuous cursing but mellow skies,
Her turbulent voices but yet melodious sighs,
Her ominous clouds but rainbowed aftermath,
Her speaking through the tempest's wrath,

"Come and touch the rainbow
And feel the rites of the skies,
As they dance with the devil
Then kiss the hand of heaven."

Nervous Rumblings

White puffy clouds basking in the sun,
sleeping in their cozy nooks,
floating in the azure skies,
basking in the rays of the sun,
meditating on pure thoughts
of tender violets or none at all,
of weightlessness in deep space,
alone with no arms and legs to
move them along, just smiling,
relaxing, and drifting in the abyss,

ahead of the approaching tempest
with its marauding eyes and battle axes,
racing through the nervous skies
upon flying dinosaurs with smoke
streaming out of their lungs,
lava shooting out of their mouths,
their razor teeth cutting through the haze,
their warlike eyes affixed
upon the peaceful valleys below,
chasing the terrified clouds up ahead,
watching them change their colors,
laughing at the way they twist and turn
and wrap around each other,
columns of black masses in embrace,
rubbing their tentacles
against their slimy, erotic skin,
the rites of the macabre
of the ghostly skies,

the battle of the spirits,
the tombs of the flying gnomes,
the assembly of the black angels,
the horror of their sighting,
the storming of the aerial beast,
the journey of the madness,
the dance with the devil,
the curse upon the earth,
the deeds of the skyborne witches,
and the way they turn the
peaceful skies into a sea
of nervous rumblings,

Spangled Nights

'Tis no more a nocturnal emptiness,
a sky without a mantle without a crest,
of noble heritage and noble banners,
no castles, cathedrals, or stately manors,

but a grand entrance to the spaces beyond,
a sky brought about by a magic wand,
crests of a trillion-fold in their blazing,
behind the riddled sky of nightward's raising,

shining through nocturnal canopies of the dark,
lighting up the sky from a kindled spark,
a journey into the spangled nights of wonder,
fragments of sorted gems cast out asunder,
a floating with the planets and the quiet nights,
we are taken by the poetry of the busy skies,
and the mystery of the night with enchanted sighs.

The Pits of Wizardry

Magic spilling out of the cold cold abyss
from the bowels of the mystic earth,
the brewing of the cryptic witches
the burning of the holy scriptures,
or the building of the scaffold to heaven,
the righteous tainted with evil thoughts,
the rising of the saints of the sun
that will peak through the tattered clouds,
or the daggers from the eyes of the beast
from the holes of the enigmatic earth,
the pits of wizardry down inside
mixing a brew that will govern the earth
and spread its good will or enmity throughout
to see what the new morn has in store
when the day brings up the wizard's brew
and lifts it up into the clean and sacred sky.

"Oh sun, thou God of light and darkness,
come forth through thy pastel colored clouds
that you painted with your feathery brushes.
Rain on what needs the raining.
Shine on what needs thy exultating powers.
Cast out the evil from the witch's brewing.
Be careful of the trees in the forest.
Be merciful to the earth's vulnerability.
Nurture the fragile crops in the fields.
Be kind to the ships on the high seas.
Make their voyage safe and sound.
Exercise thy power in a civil manner,
we beseech of thee."

Heavy Metal

Screaming sounds from Satan's wrath
Revelations sing to the aftermath
Music begs for the Devil's kiss
While wandering deep into the abyss

On the edge of tranquil spirits
Calls on rage to what befits
Hell is swelling while heaven shrinks
Witch's brew for savory drinks

Music filters into quiet dreams
Heavy rousting for all it seems
Beauty turns a different color
Sparkling reds stripped naked to duller

Blood runs freely as they come to fight
Adrenalin rushes on to take flight
Music gets inside and stirs up the warrior
Hail to the chief, the mighty conqueror
If the pen is mightier than the sword
Then how does heavy metal rank?

The Travels

A travel from the home of sound,
As quiet as a place inside the womb,
From a stirring of the listless tides,
A quiet thunder into a sweeter air,
A note plucked on a string of the harp,
A riding with the Gods of music
Upon the backs of swiftly moving steeds
On a pilgrimage to the ears of the heart,
Racing across the crimson sunsets
Through rose scented conduits,
Along an exotic path to an exotic isle,
To a sacred place where the spirit lives,
A blending with other notes into a family
Of another name but on the same mission,
The same softening of the hearts of iron,
The anti-lovers who
Submit to the power of music,
Who built their universe on grounds of stone,
But whose knees weaken like a virgin's kiss
Upon her launching out into the sea of love,
And her drifting wherever love leads her to,
Where the music dictates the feelings to be felt
And thoughts to be thought,
Where the anti-lover loses his manliness,
His identification with the lone wild beast,
Oblivious to the enchantment of sound,
The language of the music dictators,
The ones who travel through the ether

And land on a place in the heart,
A place reserved for his beguilement.

All hail to the power of music,
On its enchanting travels
That moves the immovable
And tames the wild beast.

That Special Night

I found it deep within my soul
That power, that steaming current on the go
Turning my timid spirit into a rage
My life into a book without a page

Alien creatures moved up my spine
With charging bayonets up to the rhyme
An iron poem dug its way out
And clung to my heart thereabout

Where celestial melodies reigned supreme
Where earth became an alien dream
I climbed mountain peaks to see what I saw
As golden harps sang to me in my awe

Beauty with its rhymes smiling at me
Sunsets drifting as far as I could see
Infinity looking back at me in the mirror
All dressed up in frankincense and myrrh

She smiled and said I was the chosen one
To inherit all her strength and then some
That I will fly back to earth with a melody
Locked in my heart in its drifting slowly

I played my solo that night like never before
The Gods of music filled me and every pore

Beauty was crammed into all my empty spaces
Took me into grand palaces and all splendid places
That special night will forever stay with me
In my memory, that sacred eternal sea

Music Slaves

Those floating eyes up in the sky
Sounds looking for a place to land
Eager vagabonds in their wandering
And strolling minstrels on a maiden voyage

Angels opened up their hearts and sang
Melodies cleansed by the dews of heaven
Virgin streams, passion unbound, joy acclaimed
Trumpets sending hope to the forsaken

A man sits at his piano and ponders
How to turn the ordinary into the extraordinary
A simple note into a celestial dream
A stream of pride into an ocean of modesty

Come to me, thy breath of heaven
Make me a slave to your every thought or whim
Servitude is a creed inscribed upon my brow
Never shall I wipe away what is written
When the wings of freedom come to take me away
I shall make sure they're of tuneful natures
I'm forever yours

The Lonely Flute

A breath of passion
Traveling through
Throbbing portals
A sigh so sweet
A song of the zephyrs

Harmony's a forgotten friend
Rejected and abandoned
Melody is too beautiful
Too fragile to touch
Would rather travel alone
A simple story
Tells it all
The lonely flute

History of the Music

Futuristic sound looks back to before
to the history of melody and rhythm,
when birds called to their mates
and the rain fell upon the tin roof
that sheltered the hovels
and offered relief from the storm.

Could it be a meditation
on the tap, tap, tapping
that inspired man to emulate it?
The deciphering of the rhythms?
Mother Nature's primal symphony?
The embracing of the sound?
Surrendering to its domineering ways?
Making an art form out of annoyance?
Letting it inspire him to
think of new rhythms,
to give them more life?
To find something to play them on?
Calling it a rhythmic evolution
in reverence to what it did to him?
Its tapping that drove him to dance?

When he listened to the birds,
did he hear every pitch and rhythm?
Did he sensitize himself
enough to embrace the sound?
Did he imagine that he was a bird?
Did he bring the sound into his heart?

Did it please him?
Did he try to mimic the sound?
Did he imagine what they were singing?
Did he put himself into the music?
Did he invent more melodies from it?
Did he hear them building upon each other?
Did he call it a melodic evolution?
Did he feel himself being a part
of the history of the music?

The Weeping Lyre

Songs wrapped around tender strings
As angels weep and heaven sings
As lyres melt into liquid love
And love swims into paradise above

Oceans mount from tears in their falling
Passions stirred from Polyhymnia's calling
Sacred songs where the rivers flow
Water sanctified where the angels go
An ode to music and its eternal voice
Where lyres weep and souls rejoice

Baton Man

Baton man with music in his fervent hands,
Sends it up and away into spirited lands,

Into unfamiliar seas upon the rocky waves,
Into rain forests and ancient virgin caves,

Guided by passion and dreams and love
And heavenly spirits that ride up above,

With melodic arms that pull you into a story
Of actions carried out to the sound of glory,

A softening of the words into a supple velvet,
An uncharted isle beneath a golden sunset,

Molding life and shaping it into a dream,
A tribute to the highest love supreme,

A glance at the Kingdom and a lingering sigh,
A sweet taste of nectar on a heavenly high,

An exotic feeling throughout every bone,
Then a horse drawn carriage to take you home,

Home to where the heart is full of music
And a maestro with a baton to make it tick.

Oh sweet music with him who guides it along,
Him with a dream that pours out of a song.

Melodic Winds

Whir-r-r-r-r-r through the forest glade
like the eerie howling of the wolves of Balladry
symphonic winds dressed up in red and black
seen through the eyes of the ears
of the enchanted beholder
the romance of the winds of the netherworld
split into pieces and singing through the branches
dirges to the dying greenery turned to brown
that lies on the caskets in the forest crypts
beautiful sadness and quixotic pondering
poetic reflections of the days of yore
vibrant green, singing gardens, life of life
raped by the warriors of the cruel seasons
knighted by the imperial beasts of the arctic
orchestral tears falling to the forest floors
the final breath of the flourishing gardens
winter's lament, an echoing theme throughout
from the crying of a flute unclad and lonely
or a sheep wandering and lost from the herd
a trembling melody unsupported by harmonic hands
a sadness blowing through the cold cold forest
a fanfare for the assembly of the arctic consul
 of the coming of the killers of the greens
a beautiful beast with snowy teeth
that break off into feathery white flakes
that dances with the wind
and hushes all sound and anxiety,
that just floats and sings in silence
a song of the melodic winds.

The Selection

From the busy skies, or bellowing streets,
or whistling winds, or forest nymphs,
or cathartic fires, or emancipated souls,
someone or something picked me out,
me among the crowded streets,
a speck hidden among the multitudes,
me a massive target, bigger than life,
to select me for what I know not,
my eyes looking at my shuffling feet,
my mind wandering into the pale blue sky,
emptied of all thought and denial,
my little self in tune with impartiality,
contented with my easy shuffling.

Then it came to me and rattled my bones,
a voice, and arrow that pierced my spine,
an epiphany that I wasn't looking for,
that blinded me and took me upon a journey.
A euphonic river flowed into my soul,
repeated verses and sonnets in my ears,
and dragged me into dark ally ways,
along stately thoroughfares,
manicured gardens, and into a lofted cathedral
where I awoke and looked around
at the new me, the me laden with heavy words,
the me with new wings to take me wherever,
and the me that I thought I would never be.

Why someone is selected is a mystery.
Poetry is a non-discriminate spirit that
looks for anyone to enter into.

A Tone Poem

Of stories told with enchanting tongues
Sweet breath of jasmine and myrrh
Through the still evening air
Into the rising sun and beauteous morn'
Riding with symphonic pulses
Shaping sounds with dancing fingers
With moods and dreams and colors aglow
Up and down through electric spines
Into molten rhetoric with open mouths
With liquid music and noble prose
Climbing into caves and touching the walls
With scepters poking through the fragile skin
Sinking down into the core of life
Pumping the blood through poetic veins
Chanting canticles with the mystery of song
Taming the lions with a gentle hand
With a mother's lullaby
A quiet song
A purring
A sigh
A tone poem called "The Sound of Silence."
"Of Whispering Winds," "Of Heaven's Bliss."
Riding into the sunset with the music Gods
Taking the music up to and beyond the stars
Making a new heaven out of heaven
A space beyond all spaces
A story of the stillness be stilled
Of nothing but the space

Echoes of Yesteryear

Echoes of yesteryear pass down in the forests
from tree to tree as the seasons progress.
They are the melodies of the whispering winds
that sing through the branches as the day begins.

An Autumn song to the falling leaves around,
 shows the colors afore the hoary winter bound.
The same song echoes through the passing years
and repeated in verse by nature's sonneteers.

Gowns of the Maples

Gowns of the Maple trees in emerald green,
in summer's garb and sunshine gleam,
in proud display post springtime's end,
keeping up with fashion's latest trend,
Maples dress up for summer's ball,
flaunting them in front of those enthralled,
 waltzing through the day and into the night,
twirling and twirling with no end in sight
until Autumn closes the door to the gala
with a tint of brown from its eager palette.

No more green colored gowns 'til next year
when the Maples dress up when summer's near.

Silent Hearts

To know without knowing
To discern without discerning
To taste without tasting
To dance without dancing

Silent hearts live in secret caves
Finding pleasure under ordinary rocks
Casting out popular sentiment
With their mystifying inherent rules

They dance without being told to dance
They dance because they are dancers
They love without being told to love
They love because they are lovers

Passion is not a book to be read
But a feeling to be felt
It is not a dream to run after
But a dream that became a body
A body that lives in the heart

An ode to that mystifying body
An ode to that overwhelming passion
An ode to that secret kept secret
An ode to that silent heart
That knows it all

Story In The Silence

Music floats and dancers ride the sound
With rolling arms and feet off the ground,
Rising with the calming like such sweet incense,
Spiraling into heaven and sinking in the silence.

With music as the story and rhythm as the guide,
We fly to forgotten places on a glorious ride.
We jump in the clouds and play with the rains
With freedom in our hands, we cast off the chains.

Dancers talk with bodies, and I with my heart.
We delineate the silence and lighten up the dark.
We interpret our stories just how we see fit
With music as our guide, the stories we transmit.

An ode to dancers and the feeling they convey,
Reach into my bones with their body sway,
A love affair with the artistry in motion,
Like the ire and calming of the shifting ocean.

An epic story told with a silent tongue,
As dancers dance and speakers speak.

Outer World Under

Secrets in the deep-sea world under
the wind-blown waves,
many fathoms under the reach of the fishermen,
further down under
 the tall, waterlogged swaying ocean gardens,
in a land of the aquatic creatures with
crusted eyes and stony gills slithering
through broken ships, house of the macabre,
covered in foul hoary green barnacles,
then so maybe further down near the abyss
where aquatic beasts rule the sea world
with no eyes nor gills nor breath,

where life is still a life but an outer world one,
a new life taken over and materialized,
capable of withstanding the water pressure,
an aquatic beast encased in titanium skin
with outer world motors inside
 propelling it or him ahead,
swimming through the maze,
an intelligence unexplored,
the life of the lifeless,
a playground of the spectral spirits,
a natural acclimation, or nothing at all,

down and down too deep to witness,
forever a deep-sea mystery,
a quixotic poem or a horror story,

a hell or an enigmatic heaven,
another world or a nothing,

forever a story to be written,
to be scrutinized or forgotten,
or a poem to be embellished upon,
but forever a secret and a mystery.

.

Outside Boy

Outside boy living in his chosen realm,
swirling with the madness in his head,
listening to the commanding voices thru the mist
and the music of the demon playing
The Aberration of the Gods of Baal,

skies of distorted angels flying in the dark,
swooping down to gather up the nightly seas
and putting them in their pockets
and playing with them with their hairy fingers,

outside boy building up the rage against the
emissaries of the kindhearted God
that live inside the realm
 of the American dream,

gloating in his superiority
 as he sits in his self-appointed seat
far above his foes that he
 cannot and will not see,
marching in proud submission
 to the devil's drums
in step with his wickedness and desires,

little boy with ripened stature
and pliant convictions
emerging from the devil's mold,
living in his fabricated home,
comes out to play in obedience

to the devil's command
as he wreaks havoc upon the masses
 and security of the children
and the American dream
 of Utopia in the world.

"Little outside boy, stay away from us."

Infernal Rivers

Rivers running wild from the infernal beast,
adrenal currents in the waters of the serpent,
baptism of the unholy one,
the birth of the rage of the wicked,
spume of the demonic disciples,
the black mountain tears running rampant
through unholy corridors,
adrenal currents of the deep
running down craggy cliffs, stony paths,
gathering up power and more power,
the powers of the sweetest taste,
the aroma of the gardens
driven by the electric winds of Gomorrah,
pleasuring the musty palate,
a force beyond all forces
 luxuriating in the pools of the adrenalin,
the magic strength that came from hell
that surged through the electric veins
instilling thoughts of evil
to be acted upon and
spread throughout the world,

oh yes, the infernal rivers born from
the works of the beast that
instilled the thrill of empowerment,
the triumph of the evil over good,
to the hills and valleys they run.

Global Congregation

Eden, Church, Temple, Mosque,
altars with different names,
one God, one spirit hovering over,
one universal chain to tie them all together,
one truth to spread into their hearts,
one love to feel and spread to their brothers,
one conscience to punish one for his evil deeds,
one family molded out of many different ones,
one unit upholding love's eternal grace,
many beliefs conferred and rationalized,
building an avenue to one result,
 the love and transmission of truth,
living up to the standards of love
before the inundation of religion;
hence, a global congregation at work
in the soul of man.

Of Missiles and Fists

Aggression sees mankind in his rage,
his quest for power in his mighty head,
his eternal plan since time began,
written on the walls of his cave
with his heart at the tip of his spear,
or his nuclear fingers at the computer,
typing out his plan of attack,
his secret arsenals
up his laundered sleeves,
his outward smiles and inward growls,
his adrenalin surging through his veins,
his pent up hostility
banging against the walls of his soul
with iron fists and heavy boots,
his frustrations written on his face
as they flow into his spirit
with their venom increasing the pain
as they reach every crevasse of his soul,
his proud friend that spurs him into action,
who commends him for the job well done,
his pride that goes with him to the mount,
his long lost feeling that keeps him awake,
his yearnings for that adrenalin surge,
living with that suppressed love
of war and mortality,
that numbing that crept into his fiery spirit
and made him into a
frustrated man of peace,

a man with missiles and fists
and the employment of them
swirling through his head,
still waiting in the wings.

Ice

Of your deceptions
And frigid environs
You can't live among
Smiling faces and warm climes
You dance with the devil and
Disguise yourself with sure footing
Your surface is as
Smooth as a baby's skin
As it glistens in the afternoon sun
And you gloat over your treachery
With falling bodies and smashing cars

You reach out and smother all the flowers
Until the last breath escapes from their home
The bees succumb to your frozen madness
And to your cold, cold hands
With nowhere to go but to bed

All vegetation turns to ash and you laugh
As if life were a toy for you to play with
And you were a child of the devil
Or a witch stirring up a deathly brew

Your slender bodies hang from the roof tops
And your perilous beauty glistens in the sun
While your spears point at
Those who pass underneath
As if you were sentries guarding the castle

You are alive when all else is dead
And you are dead when all else is alive
You live among the musty tombs
The cold, cold life that is not life
You are all dressed up in
Death's finest raiment
You are the ice,
That beautiful deadly ice

Sea of Treachery

Mother Nature of two faces,
seas with glassy roofs and easy gaits,
seas with melodic whispers
 and rhythmic rolling,

then seas of the swirling labyrinth,
victims of the Gods of the wind,
the Tempest showing its seven ugly heads,
sons of Neptune with contorted faces
dictating the motion of the waters,
 taking over ownership of the seas
with wayward currents, establishing new laws,
the cadence of nature in a frenzy,
the easiness of motion disturbed,
harmony of the waters running amuck,
moderation of the elements undone
for the pathway of the fisherman to sail upon,
but the journey must be done.

The quota must be filled.
The crabs must be caught
come hell or high water.

The war with the devil's breath,
the disruption of the devil's flow
in defiance against the new command,
and the will to keep on fighting
is ingrained in the spirit of the true crabber.
His livelihood depends upon his perseverance.
The task ahead is his mountain to climb
and the Tempest is his enemy to subdue.

Spears in the Mind

Spears readied to slaughter the neighbor's pig
from outside his cave; hence,
the dawning of the age of warfare,
then warriors on their steeds charging
in the heat of the battle
with their bloody spears outstretched,

writers stationed at their desks
with spears in their cathartic pens,
imaginary battles waged in their thoughts,
their passion running, aggression carried out,
spilling their thoughts onto the parchment,
playing war with no enemy to fear,
no fear of retaliation,
an easy victory gained,

but a war in the soul waged,
spears ingrained in the minds
of the youths in their carefree days,
an enemy inherited through the restlessness,
the maturation of the body but not the mind,
the peace in the soul irrelevant; therefore, unsought,
the satisfaction of the senses gained with
the sweet rivers of the adrenalin running,
the thrill of their effect employed,
the outcome of their actions prone to vengeance,
the state of the world as it has always
 been and will ever be
until . . . .

The Blitz

All is calm, all is easy, all is sound.
The pathway of the Saga is clear and precise.
The deck hands under Jake's command
are singing and pulling up the sated pods.
The crabs are clean and enormous in size.
The boat is riding on the rhythm of the waves
in perfect cadence to the swells and crests,
swaying from the nautical engines
under the deep blue sea
that pump the rhythms to steady the pulse,
the same as in ancient times and times of now,
carving out a pathway for the fishermen,
lulling them from side to side in a steady pulse
like putting a baby to sleep in mother's arms.

Oh what a fine day to be on the Bering Sea
until the human clouds see them dancing below,
transferring their jealousy and anger to the ship,
calling on their dark side to take control,
blitzing them with a ferocious attack,
calling on a rogue wave to upset
 the peace and harmony,
to dash the starboard side of the ship
and go against the poetic motion of the waves
like humans do when they act upon their jealousy.

"Roll over the side and maim those men on deck,
ye mighty rogue wave that I sent to the Saga.

Show them who the Conquistador of the Sea is.
I am the Dark Lord of the Tempest's mind and soul.
Beat the hell out of them and make them cry.
Why should they be so happy when I'm so miserable?
My sea is my playground and they are the intruders.
Do not trespass upon my waters again."

Requiem for a Soldier

Lie in peace thy defender of freedom
who died upholding the laws of martyrdom
 that's engraved in the hearts of all fighting men
who fought like hell til the very end.

He rests his bones in the forgiving ground
and lies still without making a sound
as his soul marches up to the glorious Kingdom
to the beat of a convalescing drum
where all foes and warriors sup at the table
where peace is restored and love enabled.

Rivers of Destiny

Rivers flowing into predestined places
from enigmatic sources to their chosen ends,
waters contaminated from the devil's mount,
adrenalin surging and flooding the senses,
rivers gaining speed and empowering the spirit,
singing battle hymns and stirring the blood,
pumping it through the purple maze
and sending it over the waterfalls
into the basement of the heart,
 up through the heat of the eyes,
the ire of the risen beast
and into the spirit of the evil doer.

And rivers with their foreboding sirens
 flowing into predestined places
from the grace of God,
 the paradise up on the mount
where the pure waters form and concur,
where they look out and plot their course,
their divine flowing that touches the heart
with teary eyes that can see
 affliction and helplessness,
with sinewy fingers that can knead the mountains
until they become pliant and yielding,
with hands that can lift rubble off of broken bodies
from the spirited waters that flow inside,
the adrenalin anointed by the grace of God,
the adrenalin that forms from the dews of heaven
and flows in the rivers of mercy

into the hearts of the merciful,
the God chosen ones who can see into others
and feel a breath of despair.

Lure of the Words

Words dressed in red satin with perfumed breath,
flowing out of volcanos from the foregoing left,
dipped in honey and alluring spices anew,
head right and travel onto Lyrical Avenue.

With their skirts up high and voices low,
calling for another to mingle and grow,
they melt into each other through the starry mist
and recite alluring sonnets sealed with a kiss.

Led by their loneliness and exalting needs,
they rise up and mount their flying steeds,
searching for a new life and a new enchantment,
a new paradise in their new encampment.

They lure other words to come out and play
and make their thoughts break loose and sway,
adding on and pushing them up higher
as they climb up the mount with words on fire.

They form a scaffold up to the lower empyrean
and lead each other into a fervid dream
and see the heavens unfastening and breathing
and arrows and flowers in the gleaming.

The poem is written, but the end never ends.
It circulates through the hollows of the abyss.

Love's Universal Travels

Of love's fragile spirit travelling from
its sacred womb with velvet walls,
from cathedrals floating within the empyrean
with delicate windows and pristine rooms,
its pastel colors gleaming the naked sky,
love so pure, so influential, so sapient, so earnest,
revealing itself in the human heart,
suffusing it with a new sensation,
bringing clarity to all uncertain truths,
building a new man from the
frame-work of the old,

universal love that comes to everyone,
man and woman and their gender uncertainties,
love that needs their attention, acknowledgement,
   awareness, sincerity, and reciprocation,
love that stops its flowing through no one,
in rivers of inflexibility and determination,
that doesn't know the meaning of prejudgment,
that flows above the cellars of character.

Love lifts us up to another plain
and reveals life's innermost secrets.
It shows us the smiles of the most holy
and instills his feelings into us.
It sweeps us up into its rivers
and carries us through love's secret doors
and into love's home of no name,
no language, no judgment, no segregation,
just a home filled with pure air.

Love Interpreted

As love, the commanding spirit on earth, the glue that holds civility together, the only "religion" continues on its mission on earth: its roots are trying to be undermined by interpretation. Instead of it being a feeling in the heart, it has been scrutinized by religious leaders; henceforth, the origin of religion. Where love was once an undivided spirit, it has become divided into segments; Jewish Love, Protestant Love, Methodist Love, Islamic Love, Catholic Love, and etc.; love meant for a certain kind of people. So can only these select people find it and become emissaries of it?

How can anyone scrutinize love and break it into segments? It is a power that remains a self- contained power no matter how it is interpreted. It is that feeling in the heart that God implanted and the feeling that man became exalted by and desired to prolong that feeling as long as possible. To me, love is the consecration of religion. Religion was invented by man, the same man that felt the undivided power of love, then tried to divide it.

Love in the Autumn

As the new love bit into the loin,
a primal love coated with scented herbs
that took us into the wilds
that led the way through the rusty corridors
with flaming torches
 extinguished after the love grew old,
the freshness blew away with summer's wind
as it settled down into autumn's yard.

It breathed a new breath that resurrected
from the ashes of the love burned out,
the love emptied of primal urges,
the wildness that brought us to
the relinquishment of the mind
for the sake of the feeling,
the torch that extinguished with the
chronicles of time.

Here we are devoid of the blindness
that took over from love's first bite,
the call of the jungle, the untouched foilage,
the heavy streams, the pelting rain,
the veil that dropped over our wide eyes,
the urge that took over our desires,
that commanded us to follow its ways
and led us to our losing of ourselves
for the sake of love to let its
power devour us.

Here we are in the autumn of love,
back on the ground so we can feel
the stones under our tender feet
as the biting wind blew us back to earth,
our new land that all lovers have
to return to.

Our new love is a different love.,
a wanting and a need to
 give unto each other,
 and a moral obligation to fulfill
our pledge we made as we
came back to earth.

So here we are, emissaries of the
guidelines of love and the keepers
of love's sacred mandates
for the sake of future generations.

Wave

A child of the everlasting tides,
born of the restless seas,
in a place of mystery and darkness,
on a mindless mission,
a formless entity
under the influence of a larger body,
born on the fifth day of creation,
put in eternal motion
by Neptunian hands to ever flow
and ride "til it kisses the shore,
from an ancient engine that never tires,
that moves the all powerful tides
that look up to Father Moon,
that sends its children to the surface
to join the others or act on their own,
to look at the moody skies and
their custom-made clouds,
their easy drifting
or nefarious swarming,
their intimacies with the devil,
those little children who grew up
to decide the fate of the ships,
to pull them down to their graves
or let them ride on top of the crests
and dive into the swells
until the rainbows come out and play.

They dance with their skirts up high
to the tempo of the whimsical wind.

They roll up to the shore
on the backs of their brothers and sisters.
They churn over and over as they
kiss the sand and look back at the sea,
then return to the calm until they
become another seed to be born again
at the mercy of the tides
and become another wave.

The Shedding

The pulse of summer gets old and weak
from the climbing up high to Aesta's Peak,
our Autumn Goddess sporting her fading green
with her limbs all smothered in a hoary cream.

She kisses goodbye to the proud standing trees
in their gowns in green that flow in the breeze.
They shed their emeralds for the impending cold
as autumn nears in time for the snow.
As she succumbs to the grips of Boreal,
she fades away until his summery call.

Transmission of Morals

From the Utopian spirit of yesteryear,
From up higher than the upper stratosphere,
From trumpets heralding a moral plan,
Sounding forth from a sacred land,
The foundation of fatherhood is formed.
For he must abide by the rules set forth
And make them instinctive to stay on course.
He must remain under their control
And teach his children not to break the mold.

The transmission of morals
 is for the preservation of a righteous family
and subsequently a Utopian society.

Keepers of the Sun

From my abode and
through the window,
I look up higher
than the tallest tree
where heaven commences
and my sight terminates
somewhere between earth and sky,
at the boundary of
the real and the abstract where the
giants draw the sun out of the earth
and marvel at its glossiness.

With their arms of steel extended
and their hands encased in gold,
they hold the ball of flames over
their heads and huddle
under the warmth.
They gather the clouds to their torsos
to shield their nakedness.
They look to the west
and plot their course.
They move their sluggish bodies
ever so slowly.
They cleave to the firmament
on their westward journey
until it's time to go to bed.

They become sorcerers at night
as they drift through the solid earth

with the sun still in their grasp.
They sink down to the devil's quarters
as they slide through the solid rocks.

They emerge early in the morn again
with the devil's blood in their nostrils
and a plan to assemble the clouds and
watch them release their fury upon
the earth or whether to throw them away
and smile, those giants of the sky,
tyrants of the air, voodoos in the wind,
beasts of the clouds, keepers of the sun.

The Drums of Glory

"Sound the fife and drums of glory
ye brigade of fighting men times forty.
Give 'em all you got and then some more.
Reach into your gut and then will thou soar,
reaching Triumphant Mountain you shall climb.
Then at the top you can say, ""It is mine.""

I am one of many who fought their way up.
We all did it and reached down into our gut.
Armies are a thousand men to act as one,
our goal to reach before the day is done.
For the many of our foes that are still there,
we shall out number them in battle flair.

But for some who didn't make it to the top,
upon their climb, to the dust they dropped,
we pay homage to them on this special day,
in memory of them who fell by the way,
our service men who fought 'til the end
and died for our freedom, our bravehearted friend.
Thank you, thank you, thank you, thank you.

Faith

On a cold damp night
Faith in a warming voice
Arrived at my doorstep
Like the invisible wind

Though I couldn't see it
I could feel its presence
Its soft soothing hands
Its noble smiles

In the face of the tempest
We climbed the ladder together
To that glorious Kingdom
Up high in the sky

In Slow Motion

As my sub-conscious took over and my spirit sped toward the land of dreams, my new world spoke to me in a clear and convincing voice, "Trust me, my friend. When you awaken I will help you get through your new day. Do not be alarmed, because I have nothing but good intentions toward you. I will not leave you during your waking hours and will remain at your side through the day."

When morning came, I went through my usual ritual of getting ready to go downstairs. Then while I was eating my breakfast, I looked out the window. There was a humming bird out there sipping the nectar out of the tree blossoms. I could see his wings flapping and count the number of repetitions. Their movements were like the hands of a flamenco dancer caressing the shape and sound of the music. It seemed that his time had slowed down and mine was still at the usual pace.

I got my call up from the AAA Team yesterday. The third baseman broke his leg and I had to replace him. I was a bundle of nerves. If I made a good impression, I would be able to stick around much longer. The traffic on the way to the ball park was in super slow motion, or maybe that was my new world taking its effect on me. I was still nervous when I got out of the car and made my way to the stadium, even while I was sitting on the bench in the dugout.

The score was tied 14 – 14 in the eleventh inning when I got my call to pinch hit. I grabbed a bat and ran out on the field to the on-deck circle. After Wilson was called out on strikes, it was my turn to hit. The pitcher starred at me like I was his child and proceeded to fire the ball at me. The ball took forever to get to me and I could clearly see the rotation on it and knew exactly where it was going to end up. It was a 105 MPH fast ball, but to me it was traveling 2 MPH. I could hear it speaking to me, "I'm here for you. I am your slave. Do what you wish to me. I see your heart pumping through your chest and the blood surging through your veins. I sympathize with you. I want to see the smile on your face as you hit me out of the park. I'll tell you when it's time to swing at me. O.K. Now."

I swung as hard as I could. The ball sailed out of the park and landed about 500 feet from home plate. The newspapers said that was the longest home run that was ever hit in the stadium. That gave me the incentive to keep working hard every day to stay in the big leagues. That was the start of my glorious career in baseball; thanks to the dream I had that night.

Vacuum Cleaners on High

Witches anew are the dudes of the now
on vacuum cleaners up high somehow.
They get up off their skinny out-dated brooms
and sail away up to the many moons;
no more sleeping, weeping, or serious sweeping,
but now swooping, shooting, looping, and leaping.

Skinny brooms are of the tushie digger-inner kind,
like trying to ride on a skinny porcupine;
where comfort is the way to fly today,
vacuum cleaner witches can go out and play
and sweep the moon if they so desire.

The Atonement

The man was left off easy for what he had done. All those he stole from would have liked to see him pay back the money, but since he spent it all on drugs he had none left. The judge only demanded that he was to serve one hundred hours of community service.

There was a church around the corner that needed the sanctuary painted, so he was sent over to help paint it. All the plaster on the walls and high ceiling was cracked and the paint was peeling off. The painters were glad to see him, because they needed somebody to do the scraping, caulking, and all the rest of the dirty work. He tried to convince them that he was afraid of heights, but they just laughed at him, so up the scaffold he climbed. On his way up, there was a portrait of Jesus above the altar that kept staring at him as he stared back at it. "What are you looking at?" he thought to himself. "I don't give a damn about you, and don't care if you give a damn about me. When this job is over, I don't ever want to see you or think about you again."

When the day was over, he was exhausted. He went back to the room he rented above the tavern, drank a beer, laid his head upon the pillow, and fell fast asleep. The work that he did tired him all out. The next morning he was up again, ready to go to work. He picked up his daily diary that he always wrote in, then off to work he went. He was used to writing things down, like who owed him money for the drugs he sold to them. He also liked to keep track of what he did and how he felt about things.

When he arrived at the job, the painters were kidding him, "Whatsa matter? That little bitty work ya did yesterday got you all tired out? Ah-h, you poor ba-by." Back up the scaffold he climbed again. As he stared at the portrait of Jesus, he wasn't so bitter this time. It seemed that everybody was against him except Jesus. At least he had one friend. Every day he saw him, he liked him better.   He seemed to enjoy the work a little more each day. It was like a different person was climbing up that scaffold. He got to enjoy the fellowship with the painters. When he came to work, he was so enthusiastic about getting started. After work, he stayed in the sanctuary and read the bible.

One night after he got home from work, he reached in his pocket to get his diary, but it wasn't there. He hoped it fell out at the church. He was desperate to write something down, so he just wrote it on a napkin until he got to work the next day, his last day.

When he arrived at work, the priest saw him and invited him to come into his office. "Oh no," he thought. "I did something wrong." "Have a seat," he said. "Did you lose something?" "Y-yes, I did, Father Murphy. It was a diary I keep with me." "Yes I know. Hear it is. Do you want to read some of it to me?" "O.K," I said.

"As I saw Jesus for the first time, I blamed God for the life that was given to me. After seeing his portrait every day, I could hear him saying that he was always my friend no matter what I did. The fast and easy life that I lived drove me away from him. Only hard work is the remedy to restore the faith in myself and God. Since labor is in loving God, whose dream was for everyone to be diligent, I do it to bind myself to him and to others."

The next Sunday for the sermon, he read some of his diary to the congregation. It was beautiful. He became a faithful member and gladly went about his work, painting, fixing things, and giving everything he could give. His atonement was in deed successful.

The Transcended

It was a dreary day in the little village by the river. Doom was written in the ugly gray clouds that shrouded the mountain peaks. The cold mist was circling about, and the wind was digging into the bones of the villagers with its razor teeth, and sending a chill up their spines. Death was in the air as I lay there on my deathbed about to meet my maker. The cancer had taken up residence in my body as I lay there in agony. The pain killers had worn off and left me pleading for my life to end. My relatives were sobbing as they had gathered around my bed.

Then at 5:36 PM, I breathed my final breath. At last I was free. I looked down and saw myself lying on the bed amongst the mourners. Then I saw a bright light as I floated out of the room. I was curious to find out where it came from. As I ascended to the skies, I could see things that weren't there before. That seemingly emptiness in space was a busy thoroughfare with spirits and humanity floating across the firmament. Voices that sounded like sweet music were filling the air. Angels were by my side, guiding me along the way. The dread of death was no dread at all.

I saw a Hindu man floating. I asked him if we were going to heaven, and he said in his native tongue, which I could understand. "I am just a spirit in transition, looking for a new birth. I learned from the Bhagavad-Gita that I will be reincarnated upon my death. My salvation will come soon and I will be absorbed with Brahman. I could understand the Hindu language, as I could see and understand everything in this new environment that I'm in. I could talk to a bird that told me it will go into a horse's body. There are no conflicts of beliefs here, because everyone is rewarded by his dedication to his own belief.

I met a Muslim on the way. He told me he was ready to go into his eternal paradise from what the Koran had taught him. He was rewarded for his dedication to his faith. He will be resurrected shortly. The Jewish man told me he will be physically resurrected and will live forever with God. I met a Buddhist that told me that he has achieved Nirvana and has no desire to go anywhere else.

I thought that my restlessness would cause me to become bored and lonely, but the joy of pure love replaced any anxiety that I would feel. I thought that heaven would become too common-place and that I would want to be somewhere else, but love and God made me contented with where I am. Boredom is only for those dissatisfied with themselves. They always think that another environment would be more suitable, but contentment is only a place in the heart.

Dear Lord, when it is time for me to go, please do not change your plan for me. I am completely in your custody. Do to me what you will.

Guns of the Ostracized

Everyone seeks comfort; someone or some group to enjoy being with to share the humor and joy. He must also have someone to share and rationalize his ideas with. He must have someone to listen to him. He must acquire a sense of civility from other peoples' input. He must know the importance of group interaction, how to listen to others and feel the bond between them. He must learn that others have a certain knowledge of something that he doesn't have and shouldn't resent them for it. He must learn to respect them and recognize his place in the social world. He can't look at them as being domineering because they aren't. They can learn certain things from him also. He can't let himself become bitter and resentful because of his inferiority. He can't let it fester in his mind and want to do something to get even and gain a false sense of superiority.

He can't disassociate himself from them. He needs them to learn from and be comfortable with. He can't let his resentment control his actions. In order to get even with them, he must accept who he is and work toward a civil way to earn his respect. He can't gain it through violence. He will never know what it is to love and be loved or to admire and be admired. He will miss out on the main ingredients of life; the love and friendship. If he chooses violence against others, he deserves the violence commited against himself. Violence could never solve any social problem. It is just the evil calling for a retaliation of more evil.

Guns for the Ostracized is the creed of the wicked. The ways of the righteous is the noble advancement of the simple minded; of one's inferiority calling for his introspection in order to advance himself through a communal need.

Revisions

Your silent language hailed me from beyond the seas and offered me its wings above the roar of the angry waters. I heard your call though it was silent but ever so expressive. Your silent lips remained as still as the midst that hangs over the valley, but your emotions conveyed all the complexities of your busy heart. Your utterances confused that which has been determined, while your silence is still the language of the spirit, that messenger of truth that forever prevails.

Our expressions are the windows to our hearts. Truth, with gavel in hand, sits at the bench judging whether the eyes are in unison with the words being spoken. It is easy to tell a lie, but hard to cover it up. Our silent language reveals the truth and all its revisions of it.

Linear Stimuli

What kind of line are you? Do you curve around and entangle yourself with yourself with no end to your travels? Do you tell a story about beauty, the way it flaunts itself in all its glory? Are you bestowed with rich colors and curves that move with grace and play upon feelings?

Do you lie upon a pedestal and encompass yourself in the form of a woman? Do you inspire artists to move their brushes with grace and passion? Do you take the one who gazes upon you to exotic places that speak to him with the language of the Gods?

Are you straight, vertical, and horizontal that puts facts and information in their proper places where the Gods are merely muted spectators that hibernate back into their caves? Is brevity you mode of speech that bestills the heart and expands the intellect? Is life black and white, or is it imbued with a rose colored radiance?

What we read into the lines affects how we are moved by them. Stimulation isn't so much as how we choose it, but how it chooses us.

Writers That We Are

Everybody dreams. Some forget about them. Some try to forget but they can't. Some are afraid of them. Some don't know how valuable they are. Some don't think they need to understand them. They don't know what they are capable of. They don't care to know and just go on not knowing how to love themselves and escape from their boredom.

We writers hold the key to keep our enthusiasm of life. It is not something that we want to get over with and just wait out the years until they are no longer with us. It is our precious possession that we inherit, and we are able to find out how precious it is. We know how to build our self-esteem. We know how to exalt ourselves through our writing. We know how to tap into our creative self, our secret treasure chest that lies within us. We know how to utilize our God given talent to the best of our ability. We know how boredom can affect us and we know how to fight it off. We create a passion for life through our enthusiasm.

Our mission in life is something that we can hold dear to us. Our writing is something that stays within us and keeps on going. It is not a task to get over with, but a collection of thoughts that have to get out of our loving selves. Our words are the expansion of our minds and the language of our hearts.

We are wonderful so we are
We are valuable so we are
We are precious so we are
We are intelligent so we are
We are writers so we are